Intentional Money

The Modern Woman's Guide to Building Wealth, Purpose, and Peace

Leah Hadley, AFC, CDFA

For my mom, Delle Rayner. My first teacher. My first believer. The woman who showed me that following your heart and building your future aren't two different paths. They're the same one.

Contents

Chapter 1

Rethinking Money

Why the Old Way Isn't Working

WHEN I FIRST STOOD at the edge of real money responsibility, I believed wealth meant bigger numbers. A bigger paycheck. A stronger balance sheet. Proof on paper that I was doing things right. I chased promotions, dinners at nice restaurants, the quiet validation of being seen as successful. I absorbed the unspoken rules early: Work hard, keep climbing, don't fall behind.

The more I earned, the more I spent trying to prove, mostly to myself, that I was on track.

From the outside, it looked like progress. From the inside, it felt like pressure.

There was always another rung to reach for. Another benchmark to hit. Another version of "enough" that stayed just out of reach. I wore the armor of competence and confidence, but underneath it lived a steady hum of anxiety.

Am I keeping up? Am I doing this right? Why doesn't this feel as secure as it's supposed to?

I didn't have language for it then, but I was chasing someone else's definition of success. And it was quietly exhausting me.

For many women, this shows up quietly rather than dramatically. You hit milestones that were supposed to feel satisfying, but the relief is short-lived. You earn more, yet the anxiety doesn't soften. You spend in ways that look reasonable on paper, but something still feels off. You stay busy, productive, responsible, yet oddly disconnected from a sense of arrival. The life you're building looks successful from the outside, but inside there's a persistent question you can't quite shake: *Is this really what all this effort is for?*

When that question goes unanswered for too long, money becomes a source of pressure rather than support. Not because you're doing anything wrong, but because you're measuring your life against a standard you never consciously chose.

The moment that finally cracked something open wasn't dramatic. It didn't involve a financial crisis or a major life event. It was a photo. A friend posted a gleaming picture of a new SUV, the comments full of celebration and admiration. I felt the familiar flicker of comparison, but beneath it was something else.

Fatigue.

A deep, unmistakable tiredness of chasing a version of wealth that didn't match the life I wanted.

That was the first time I asked myself a different question. Not *How do I get more?* but *What would enough actually look like for me?*

The answer surprised me. It wasn't tied to a number. It wasn't a title or an upgrade. It had nothing to do with keeping up. It was about how my days felt. Whether I had space to breathe. Whether I could handle a curveball without panic. Whether my money supported the people and values that mattered most to me instead of pulling me away from them.

That question marked the beginning of a new money story, one where money served a meaningful life instead of defining it. I don't separate money from life. I don't think that's how it works.

I didn't arrive at that realization all at once. It deepened over years of sitting across from women in moments of profound financial disruption. Divorce, career pivots, caregiving transitions, the quiet reckoning of realizing the plan they'd been following wasn't leading where they thought it would. Different circumstances, same undertone.

They weren't failing at money. The system they'd been taught to follow simply wasn't built for their lives.

The old playbook promised certainty. Earn steadily, save consistently, invest early, and everything will work out. But that promise assumes a linear life. Predictable income. Predictable health. Predictable relationships. Predictable time.

Life is not predictable.

Money doesn't exist in a vacuum. It's shaped by identity, emotion, responsibility, and change. And when those realities collide with a rigid system, something has got to give. Too often, it's our sense of safety, confidence, or self-trust.

For women, the gap between the playbook and reality is even wider. The wage gap compounds quietly over decades. Time spent caregiving creates invisible gaps in earnings, retirement savings, and Social Security benefits. Longevity means stretching resources further, often with less margin for error. These aren't exceptions. They are common experiences.

Yet most financial advice treats them as footnotes instead of foundational truths.

But the real barrier isn't missing information. It's the stories we've inherited about money and worth.

Stories that say security comes from staying quiet and being grateful. Stories that equate ambition with selfishness. Stories that reward endurance while discouraging boundaries.

We learn early, often unconsciously, that wanting ease is indulgent. That asking for more is risky. That stability is something you earn by tolerating discomfort. We comply. We push through. We normalize stress. And we call it responsibility.

Over time, fear becomes background noise. We confuse busyness with progress. We accept arrangements that drain us because they look stable on paper. When life throws us a detour, a health issue, a job loss, or a relationship shift, the system cracks, leaving us scrambling at the exact moment we need clarity most.

My real breakthrough didn't come from another spreadsheet or strategy. It came from a quieter internal shift: The conviction that money should be a tool for living, not a constant source of pressure.

That shift required starting somewhere different.

It required clarity.

Clarity isn't about judgment or perfection. It's about honestly seeing where you are, what you value, what you're tolerating, and what you're afraid to name. Until you can see those things clearly, every financial decision feels reactive.

I began with a simple practice that I now use with clients. I call it vision mapping, but it's less about goals and more about grounding.

I asked myself:

What do I want my life to feel like in a year?

In five years?

In ten?

Not what do I want to own, not what should I want, but what kind of days do I want to wake up to? What do I want to protect? What do I want more space for?

The answers weren't flashy. They were honest. Time with family. Energy instead of constant depletion. The ability to say no without fear. The confidence to handle change without unraveling.

Money, I realized, wasn't the point. The support system was.

From clarity came alignment. Core values emerged. Not as aspirational words, but as practical guardrails. Family. Independence. Learning. Service. Health. These became filters. If a decision supported them, it moved forward. If it didn't, it deserved reconsideration.

Slowly, intentionally, my money choices began to reflect my life instead of competing with it.

That alignment demanded a mindset shift. The old scripts didn't disappear overnight. They softened as I replaced them with something truer. *Money is a tool I can learn to use. I don't need to get it perfect to move forward. I'm allowed to build wealth in a way that honors who I am.*

From there, action became possible. Not dramatic action. Sustainable action. Small habits. Regular check-ins. Honest conversations. Systems that supported real life instead of idealized versions of it.

That's the work this book is here to guide you through.

If something in this chapter feels familiar, that's not a coincidence. You don't need to be in crisis to need a new approach. You just need to notice that the old one isn't working the way you hoped it would.

Let's briefly and intentionally pause here. Take a breath.

Think about the messages you learned about money growing up. Not the formal lessons. The offhand comments, the tone, the rules no one ever said out loud.

Where do those messages still show up in your life today? And where do they feel outdated, heavy, or misaligned with who you are now?

You don't need to fix anything yet. You don't need answers. Just noticing where the old story no longer fits is enough for now.

Because everything we build next begins with this moment of honesty.

The old money story doesn't get to decide what happens next. You do.

Chapter 2

The Six Pillars of the Intentional Money Method

If you paused at the end of Chapter 1 and sat with the question—*What would the life I want require if money supported it?*—you may have felt something stir. Maybe clarity. Maybe discomfort. Maybe a quiet sense of possibility mixed with uncertainty.

That's not a sign you're doing this wrong. That's the work beginning.

You don't need answers yet. You don't need a perfect plan. What you need is a structure that can hold whatever you're carrying right now and help you move forward without overwhelm. That's what the six pillars are designed to do.

I didn't create this framework in a moment of inspiration or from a single breakthrough. It emerged slowly, through years of listening to my own experience and through the stories of women navigating money during divorce, career transitions, caregiving seasons, reinvention after burnout, and moments when the life they'd been building no longer fit. Different circumstances, different details. The same underlying frustration.

They weren't short on effort. They weren't short on intelligence. They weren't failing at money. They were trying to operate without a system that reflected real life.

Most financial advice doesn't fail because it's wrong. It fails because it's incomplete.

A budget without meaning becomes a chore. A savings goal without emotional safety feels fragile. A strategy without mindset collapses under pressure.

What I kept seeing was people had pieces, but the pieces weren't connected. When one part wobbled, everything else followed. So I built a framework where nothing stands alone.

The Intentional Money Method rests on six interconnected pillars: **Clarity, Values, Mindset, Strategy, Action, and Support**.

Think of them not as steps to complete, but as supports that hold up a life. When all six are present, your financial life becomes resilient and able to adapt when things change rather than breaking apart.

Because these pillars don't operate in a straight line, this book isn't meant to be read that way either. You don't need to absorb it all at once or follow a prescribed order. This isn't a manual you're meant to master. It's a conversation you're meant to return to.

Some chapters will feel immediately relevant. Others may not land until a different season of life. That's expected. You may find yourself rereading a section months from now and noticing something new. Let that happen.

Use the chapters as touchpoints, not checkpoints. The goal isn't to "finish" this book. The goal is to build a relationship with your money that evolves as you do.

You'll notice that when something feels hard or stuck, the answer is rarely "Try harder." More often, it's a signal that attention is needed somewhere else. If investing feels overwhelming, the issue may not be risk; it may be clarity or support.

If spending feels out of control, the issue may not be discipline; it may be values or tolerations. If saving feels impossible, the issue may not income; it may be emotional safety. The pillars help you diagnose what's actually happening beneath the surface so you can respond with curiosity instead of self-criticism.

This is why the framework works as a compass, not a hammer. You're not meant to force yourself into change. You're meant to understand where alignment has loosened and gently bring it back.

Let's walk through the pillars together.

Clarity

Everything begins with clarity. Not judgment. Not shame. Just truth.

Clarity is the practice of seeing where you are right now—your income, your spending, your savings, your debt, your habits, and the emotions tied to all of it. Without clarity, every financial decision feels reactive. With clarity, you regain orientation.

Clarity doesn't ask you to fix anything. It asks you to look.

When clarity is missing, money often feels loud and exhausting. You may feel busy but unsure whether anything is improving. You might avoid opening accounts, delay decisions, or describe yourself as "bad with money" when what's really missing is visibility.

Clarity is not a onetime snapshot. It's a skill you return to whenever things feel noisy or overwhelming. When money feels stressful, clarity is often the pillar asking for attention.

Values

Once you can see where you are, the next question becomes: *Where do I want to go and why?*

Values are not aspirational words you write down once and forget. They are living filters. They guide what you say yes to, what you protect, and what you let go of.

When your earning, spending, saving, and investing reflect your values, money stops feeling adversarial and starts feeling supportive.

When this pillar is weak, decisions tend to feel heavy or guilt-ridden. You may spend money and immediately second-guess yourself or save diligently without feeling any sense of satisfaction. Without clearly named values, it's easy to default to other people's priorities and call it responsibility.

Values give direction to every other pillar. Without them, effort feels disconnected from meaning.

Mindset

Mindset is the lens through which every financial choice passes.

It's shaped by the messages you absorbed growing up, the roles you've played, and the expectations placed on you. Stories about worth, safety, and responsibility quietly influence what feels possible long before logic enters the conversation.

Mindset work isn't about positive thinking. It's about awareness.

When this pillar is underdeveloped, you may know exactly what to do but struggle to follow through. You may hesitate to negotiate, avoid investing, or downplay your progress.

Not because you're incapable, but because an old story is running in the background.

When you notice the story, you can decide whether it still deserves a voice.

Strategy

Strategy is where clarity, values, and mindset turn into a plan that fits your actual life.

This isn't about copying someone else's formula. It's about designing systems that reflect your priorities, capacity, and the season you're in. Strategy answers practical questions:

- How do I earn in a way that supports my life?

- How do I spend without guilt?

- How do I protect myself while still building for the future?

When strategy is missing, people often rely on willpower instead of systems. Things work for a while, until life gets complicated. A good strategy feels grounding, not restrictive. It creates structure without rigidity.

Action

Action is where intention meets reality. Not big, dramatic moves. Consistent ones.

Small actions repeated over time are what create momentum. Automatic transfers. Weekly check-ins. One honest conversation you've been avoiding.

When this pillar is weak, it's easy to stay stuck in planning mode. You may feel prepared, but not progressing. Action doesn't require perfection, it requires follow-through. And follow-through becomes easier when action is designed to be sustainable.

If things feel stalled or chaotic, this pillar is often where recalibration helps most.

Support

This is the pillar most people try to skip and the one that determines whether change lasts.

Support doesn't mean outsourcing responsibility. It means creating an environment where growth is easier to maintain. Support can be a mentor, a trusted partner, a community, or simply a space where money conversations are normal instead of avoided.

When support is missing, even the strongest intentions get tired. Change becomes lonely. Progress feels fragile.

This is why I created the Empowered Sisterhood. Not as a solution you need, but as an example of what support can look like. A place where women can talk about money honestly, ask questions without judgment, celebrate progress, and keep showing up even when motivation dips.

Financial change doesn't happen in isolation. It happens in relationship.

How the Pillars Work Together

These pillars aren't meant to be mastered or checked off. They work together, constantly.

- Clarity informs Values.

- Values steady Mindset.

- Mindset allows Strategy to stick.

- Strategy makes Action possible.

- Action is sustained through Support.

When one pillar weakens, the others help hold it up. When all six are present, you have a system that bends instead of breaks.

I use this framework as a compass, not a hammer. When something feels off, I don't ask, *What am I doing wrong?* I ask, *Which pillar needs attention right now?* That single question replaces shame with curiosity, and curiosity leads to better decisions.

Where to Begin

You don't need to work on all six pillars at once. You just need a place to start. As you think about them, notice which pillar made you pause. The one that felt relevant, uncomfortable, or relieved. That's your entry point.

- If it's **Clarity**, spend ten minutes writing down where you are right now. No judgment. Just facts.

- If it's **Values**, name the three things that matter most in this season and compare them to where your money is actually going.

- If it's **Mindset**, write down the first few thoughts that come up when you think about money. Those are your stories.

- If it's **Strategy**, identify one decision you've been avoiding and name what feels unclear.

- If it's **Action**, choose one small habit you could realistically do this week.

- If it's **Support**, tell one person you trust that you're thinking differently about money.

That single step is enough.

Before we move on, let me say this clearly: The pillars are not a test. They are a language. A way to understand what's happening beneath the surface so you can respond with intention instead of reaction.

You'll see these pillars woven through every chapter that follows: earning, spending, saving, investing, and giving. Because money doesn't show up in isolation. It shows up in real life.

In the next chapter, we'll begin where everything starts: intention. Not goals you feel obligated to chase, but a personal vision rooted in what matters to you.

Take a breath.

You're not behind.

You're building something that's meant to last.

Chapter 3

Setting Your Intentions and Defining Your Personal Vision

I WAKE BEFORE SUNRISE, the house quiet, coffee warm in my hands. There was a season when these mornings felt like borrowed time. An hour stolen before the real work began. I used them to scan emails, make lists, push myself forward. Progress, I told myself, meant staying in motion.

On the wall near my desk hung a list of goals I'd written years earlier. Promotions. Growth targets. Milestones that once felt urgent. Nearby was a photo of my kids from a moment I almost missed because I was already thinking about the next thing.

That photo did what the goals never could. It stopped me.

I realized I'd been moving quickly, but not intentionally.

Like many women, I learned how to be responsible, productive, and capable long before I learned how to ask myself what I wanted. I knew how to meet expectations. I knew how to push through. What I hadn't practiced was pausing long enough to decide whether the direction I was headed was one I would choose again.

We live in a culture that treats momentum as virtue. Busy is praised. Full calendars are admired. Exhaustion is quietly rewarded. And women carry this script alongside careers, caregiving, relationships, and the unspoken expectation that we should manage it all gracefully.

The result is often a life that looks successful from the outside and feels misaligned on the inside.

And then there's time.

Time doesn't wait for clarity. It keeps moving whether we're conscious of it or not. Without intention, we drift. We say yes because it's easier than explaining no. We chase what sounds respectable instead of what feels meaningful. Slowly, almost imperceptibly, we build a life we never explicitly chose.

The risk isn't making the wrong decision. It's never making a decision in the first place.

Why Intention Matters More Than Goals

Most financial advice jumps straight to goals. Save this amount. Earn that number. Retire by this age.

But goals without intention are fragile. They're easily disrupted by life changes. They lose relevance when circumstances shift. They can even trap you in a version of success that no longer fits.

Intention works differently.

Intention is about direction, not destination. It's about naming what matters enough to protect, even as life evolves. It gives your goals context. It tells your money what it's working for.

When intention is missing, money decisions feel heavy. Reactive. Disconnected. You may do all the "right" things and still feel unsettled, because the plan you're following isn't anchored to your life.

That's what I was beginning to sense in those quiet mornings. I didn't need more ambition. I needed alignment.

I stopped asking, *What should I be working toward?* And started asking, *What kind of life am I trying to build?*

Vision Mapping: A Different Starting Point

That question led me to a practice I now use with some clients. I call it vision mapping, but it's less about imagining a perfect future and more about grounding yourself in what matters now.

It starts with how you want your life to feel.

Not what you want to own. Not what you think you should want. Not what looks impressive. But the texture of your days.

I map vision across three horizons—not because life follows a neat timeline, but because perspective changes when you zoom out.

One year from now:

What do you want your days to feel like?What feels heavy right now that you want less of?What would make an ordinary Tuesday feel like a good day?

Five years from now:

What kind of work do you want to be doing?What relationships do you want to be investing in?What do you want more space for?

Ten years from now:

When you look back, what do you want to recognize?What do you want to feel proud of protecting?What do you want to know you didn't sacrifice along the way?

When I first answered these questions, the responses weren't flashy. They were honest.

Time with family.Energy instead of depletion.The ability to say no without panic.Confidence that I could handle change without unraveling.

Money wasn't the point; it was the support system.

That realization changed everything because it gave me a filter. From that point forward, financial decisions were no longer about optimization. They were about alignment.

When Intention Becomes Practical

Clarity about intention isn't abstract. It becomes practical very quickly.

Once I named what mattered, I began to notice where my life and money were quietly out of sync. Commitments that drained me. Spending that didn't reflect my values. Earning structures that made everything feel rushed.

I didn't overhaul my life. I adjusted it. I protected mornings. I simplified choices. I stopped saying yes by default. Small, meaningful shifts.

That's the power of intention. It doesn't demand dramatic change. It creates discernment.

Diane's Story: When Vision Unlocks Movement

Let me tell you about a woman I worked with. I'll call her Diane.

Diane came to me at fifty-four, recently divorced, standing in the middle of a life she didn't quite recognize. On paper, she was stable. A fair settlement. A modest pension from years in education. A house that was paid off.

But when I asked her what she wanted next, she froze.

Not because she was confused about money but because she hadn't been asked that question in decades.

For most of her adult life, Diane's financial decisions had been made in service of someone else's plan. Where to live. How to spend. When to save. Even small choices were filtered through another person's preferences.

She'd been a good partner. She'd been a good mother. She just hadn't practiced choosing.

When I introduced vision mapping, she laughed nervously. "I don't know what I want," she said. "I've never really thought about it that way."

We didn't start with five or ten years. We started with a single Tuesday.

I asked her to describe an ordinary weekday. Not a vacation or a celebration but rather one that felt good. One that felt like hers.

She was quiet for a long time.

Then she said, "I'd wake up without an alarm. I'd have coffee on the porch. I'd spend the morning doing something with my hands. Gardening, maybe. And in the afternoon,

I'd do something useful. Teach something. Help someone. Something that uses the part of me that's been dormant."

That was the first time she described her own life in her own words.

From that single Tuesday, everything else followed.

We built outward to weeks, months, and years. Her spending shifted naturally because she could finally see what didn't belong anymore. Subscriptions tied to an old life. Expenses that no longer matched her values. Commitments that drained her.

Six months later, she called me after making a decision she would have agonized over before.

"For the first time," she said, "I chose something because it fit me. Not because it was expected."

That's what intention does. It gives decisions a center of gravity.

Intention Is Not Static

One of the most important things to understand about intention is it is not something you decide once and then defend forever.

Your life will change. Your responsibilities will shift. Your capacity will expand and contract.

Intention isn't about locking yourself into a future version of yourself. It's about giving yourself a way to choose consciously instead of defaulting.

This is why intention works better than rigid goals. It flexes with you. It gives you permission to adjust without feeling like you've failed.

And it grows stronger when it's witnessed.

When Diane shared her vision with her sister, something changed. Her sister didn't fix it. She didn't critique it. She remembered it.

Months later, when Diane almost canceled a trip she'd been looking forward to, her sister said, "You told me this mattered. It still does."

That sentence carried more weight than any budget ever could.

Your Invitation

Setting intentions doesn't require a dramatic declaration. It requires honesty.

Set aside a quiet moment. Take a piece of paper and answer these three prompts slowly:

- One year from now, I want my days to feel like ________.

- Five years from now, I want my life to include _________.

- Ten years from now, I want to look back and know that I _________.

Don't worry about how the numbers will work yet. Don't worry about sounding polished.

Circle the words or themes that repeat. Those are your anchors. Those are what your money will need to support.

If you can, share your vision with someone safe. Someone who will listen without fixing. Someone who might ask you about it again.

Intention becomes real when it's spoken.

As we move into the next chapter, we'll talk about aligned earning and how the way you earn can support the life you've just named. Not through hustle or self-sacrifice, but through clarity, boundaries, and self-trust.

You don't need to see the whole path from here. You just need a direction that feels like yours. And that alone is a powerful beginning.

Chapter 4

Grow Your Income Wisely through Aligned Earning

I REMEMBER THE MOMENT I decided to stop undercharging. It wasn't dramatic. There was no single conversation that flipped a switch. It was a slow, quiet accumulation of re-alizations, each one a little louder than the last until one morning, I sat down and thought: *This doesn't reflect the work I'm doing. It doesn't reflect the value I'm creating.*

At the time, undercharging showed up as fees. But under-charging doesn't only happen in business ownership. For you, it might show up as a salary that hasn't changed in years, a role that keeps expanding without recognition, or a schedule that demands more than it gives back. The form is different, but the feeling is the same—that persistent sense that the exchange is off.

Claiming my value felt terrifying. Not because I doubted the impact of my work. I didn't. But there's a difference between knowing your contribution matters and believing you're allowed to be compensated for it without apology. I had invested years in building expertise, earning credentials, and doing complex work that most people don't think about until they urgently need it. And still, when it came time to align my income with that reality, something in me flinched.

The old script was familiar: Who are you to ask for more? What if they say no? What if you lose stability?

That script doesn't belong only to entrepreneurs. It runs just as loudly for women in salaried roles. We're taught, often implicitly, that gratitude should replace negotiation, that loyalty should outweigh leverage, and that asking for more puts us at risk of being seen as difficult or ungrateful. We wait. We accommodate. We tell ourselves we'll revisit it later.

What made this especially complicated for me was the juggling act. I was raising three kids while trying to show up fully in my work and my life. Every hour I spent doubting my worth was an hour not spent where it mattered most. That tension between earning a living and living a life became one of my clearest teachers.

I learned when your income isn't aligned with the value you create and the life you're trying to support, the cost goes far beyond money. It shows up as exhaustion. As resentment. As saying yes when you mean no. As coming home with nothing left for the people you love or the life you're building.

The real turning point didn't come from a spreadsheet or a strategy session. It came from a conversation. A woman I worked with, I'll call her Sara, came to me in the middle of a divorce. Her income had been intertwined with her husband's for over a decade. She'd stepped back from her career during the years her children were small, and when she tried to re-enter the workforce, she found herself quoting rates she'd charged years earlier. Not because the market had changed, but because she'd internalized a story about what she deserved.

We spent months untangling not just her finances but her sense of what she was allowed to ask for. When she finally raised her consulting rate, and a client said yes without hesitation, something shifted in her that went far beyond the number on the invoice. She called me afterward and said, "This is the first time anyone has helped me see my own worth clearly. Not just on paper. Inside."

That moment stayed with me—not because of what it said about her, but because of what it revealed about me. I was helping other women name their value while hesitating to fully claim my own.

That's what aligned earning means. It's not about greed. It's not about hustle or ambition for ambition's sake. It's about ensuring that the way you earn reflects the life you're trying to live and that your income gives you enough stability, flexibility, and dignity to show up fully.

Aligned earning does not require you to quit your job, start a business, or take on more than you can sustain. Those are structural choices, not moral ones. What matters is whether you're making intentional decisions about how you earn or simply accepting the default.

For a long time, I was good at my job. I met expectations. I showed up. But the true cost of my earning structure wasn't visible on any paycheck or performance review. It showed up at home. It showed up in missed moments. It showed up in a version of myself that was always a little too tired and a little too stretched. I wasn't choosing how I earned. I was tolerating it.

Earning tolerations are some of the hardest to see because they often hide behind stability. They look like roles that pay well but cost you more energy than you can sustainably give. Compensation that hasn't kept pace with your responsibilities. Schedules that leave no room to breathe. Emotional labor that's expected but never acknowledged.

You tell yourself it's fine because it's familiar, because it's better than uncertainty, because changing it would feel risky. But over time, these tolerations don't just drain income. They drain agency. They quietly teach you to accept misalignment as the price of security, until earning starts to feel like something that happens *to* you rather than something you shape.

This is where many women find themselves, regardless of employment status. If you work for someone else, you may feel boxed into a role that no longer fits your life. If you run a business, you may feel trapped by a structure you built in an earlier season. Different paths. Same risk. Confusing familiarity with alignment.

Earning isn't just about the number deposited into your account. It's about what that number costs you and what it enables. If the way you earn is quietly undermining your health, your relationships, or your sense of agency, that's not a small issue. That's a structural one.

Here's something essential to hold as we move forward. Growing your income wisely isn't only about earning more. It's about earning better. Better aligned with your energy. Better matched to your values. Better designed for the season of life you're actually in.

This matters because the way you earn today becomes the seed for everything else—how you spend, how you save, how you invest, and how resilient you are when life changes. Income isn't just cash flow. It's capacity.

The biggest obstacle most women face here isn't lack of skill or opportunity. It's misalignment between what we say we want and what we're willing to ask for or redesign. We live in a world that tells us the solution is always more. Another credential, another responsibility, another side hustle layered onto an already full life.

But for many women, the deeper fear isn't can I earn more; it's what happens if I disrupt what feels stable?

That fear becomes sharper when caregiving enters the picture, when health shifts, or when the economy feels uncertain. In those moments, it can feel safer to cling tightly to a single role or income stream, even when it no longer serves us well. Security gets outsourced to one employer, one business model, one path. And that's a fragile place to stand.

My breakthrough wasn't a new formula. It was a reframing. I began to see aligned earning as a practice grounded in value, leverage, and autonomy, regardless of how income is generated.

From that anchor came three moves that apply whether you're salaried, self-employed, or somewhere in between.

First, get clear on the value you create.

Stop defining your worth by hours, effort, or job descriptions. Start naming outcomes. Problems solved. Stability created. Time saved. Revenue protected or generated. This matters inside organizations just as much as it does in business ownership. When you can articulate impact, you change how you advocate for yourself.

Second, reduce single-point dependency.

This doesn't always mean a second job or income stream. Sometimes it means developing skills that give you leverage. Sometimes it means negotiating flexibility instead of compensation. Sometimes it means a modest supplemental income that adds resilience without draining you. The goal isn't exhaustion, it's optionality.

Third, approach negotiation as alignment, not confrontation.

Preparation replaces fear. Evidence replaces apology. Whether you're discussing compensation, scope, flexibility, or pricing, the goal isn't to demand. The goal is to present a clear case for mutual value. Negotiation becomes a conversation about sustainability rather than self-worth.

Over time, aligned earning becomes a habit. You start evaluating decisions through a different lens. Does this opportunity support the life I'm building? Does this structure honor my capacity? Does this income source create stability or quietly erode it?

Let's make this practical.

Over the next ninety days, I want you to focus on one lever you can pull to change your earning story. Just one.

If that lever is a raise, role adjustment, or renegotiation, start by documenting your actual impact over the past year. Not responsibilities. *Results.* Then practice naming them out loud. The words may feel uncomfortable at first. That discomfort is information. Stay with it.

If that lever is a supplemental income stream or business adjustment, start smaller than you think. You're not reinventing your identity this quarter. You're testing alignment. Look for the intersection of your skills, your values, and your capacity. Sustainability matters more than speed.

Before you move on, take a moment with this question: Where does the way you earn money feel fair and supportive right now? Where does it feel tight, draining, or out of sync with the life you're trying to build?

Now pick one change to make in the next few months. One conversation, one adjustment, one boundary. What would you change? You don't have to have the answers today. Just notice what comes up.

Hold this truth as you do the work. This isn't about proving anything but rather about creating enough stability and space to live your life with intention. That's the point.

Growth doesn't require dramatic leaps. It requires deliberate choices. And you are allowed to make them.

Chapter 5

Spend with Purpose: Value-Based Spending

THERE WAS A NIGHT that changed how I thought about every dollar I spent.

I'd had a week of back-to-back commitments—work deadlines, school events, and a dinner I said yes to because it felt easier than explaining no. By Friday evening, I was running on fumes. I opened our bank app to check something routine, and what I saw stopped me. A string of small charges, each one with its own quiet justification. A coffee shop here. A streaming service I'd forgotten about. A few impulse purchases tied to the kids' schedules and my own exhaustion.

None of it was reckless. All of it was automatic.

I sat there for a while, not with guilt, but with a slow, uncomfortable recognition. I hadn't been spending with purpose. I'd been spending to cope with stress, with depletion, with a life that felt fuller than it felt supportive.

That night, I wrote a sentence on a sticky note and stuck it inside my wallet: *Spend in a way that supports the life you want, or your money will quietly fund the life that drains you.*

It wasn't a budget rule. It was a truth.

The challenge with spending isn't information. We already know where money *should* go. The challenge is that spending often becomes emotional regulation long before it becomes a financial decision. It fills gaps we don't have language for yet. Relief. Reward. Control. Comfort. A sense of having something that's just for us.

We live in a world that makes this easy. One-click checkout. Endless delivery. Curated lifestyles that suggest ease is something you buy, not something you build. Many decisions are made in seconds, not in alignment.

And for women especially, there's another layer. Spending on yourself can feel selfish, even when you're the one holding everything together. Money leaks out quietly. On convenience, on treats, on small comforts that feel earned after hard days. The result is often a paycheck that should be building something meaningful but instead leaves you wondering why there never seems to be much left.

This is where Ann comes in.

Ann had a big title. A high income. The kind of career that looks impressive from the outside. When she came to me, she was frustrated because she felt like she *should* be further ahead.

"I make good money," she said. "I don't feel irresponsible. And yet my savings never seem to grow the way I expect them to."

When we looked at her spending, nothing jumped out as excessive. No dramatic splurges. No obvious red flags. But there was a steady stream of discretionary spending—daily takeout, convenience services, and frequent shopping for things she didn't need.

At first, she assumed this was a discipline issue. She talked about cutting back. Being stricter. Trying harder.

But when I asked her about her days, the story changed.

Her role had become quietly unbearable. A stressful boss. Constant urgency. A feeling of being "on" all the time. By the end of the day, she was depleted. Spending wasn't about indulgence. It was relief. Ordering in instead of cooking because she had nothing left. Buying small things online because it felt like a moment of control in a day where she had very little.

Then Ann made what looked like a lateral move. Same company. Similar title. Comparable pay. But the environment was different. A healthier manager. Clearer expectations. Fewer emotional landmines.

What happened next surprised her.

Without trying to budget harder, her discretionary spending dropped. Not because she told herself no, but because she no longer *needed* the same level of relief. She cooked more. She ordered less. She stopped buying things out of stress.

And almost immediately, her investment account started to grow.

Not because she earned more, not because she became more disciplined, but because her life stopped draining her in the same way.

Ann's story is important because it reveals something essential. **Spending patterns are often symptoms, not problems**. Before you cut expenses, it's worth asking what your spending is responding to.

When Spending Is Trying to Solve a Life Problem

One of the most common mistakes people make with spending is trying to fix it in isolation. We treat it like a behavior problem when it's often a signal problem. Spending rarely exists on its own. It's usually responding to something else that hasn't been named yet.

Sometimes spending is compensating for exhaustion. When your days are packed, your nervous system looks for shortcuts. Takeout replaces cooking. Convenience replaces intention. Not because you don't care, but because your capacity is depleted. In those seasons, cutting spending without addressing energy is like turning down the volume while the fire alarm is still going off.

Other times, spending is about identity. You buy clothes, experiences, or upgrades not because you need them, but because they help you feel like the version of yourself that you're struggling to access elsewhere. Confident. Successful. Put together. When work, relationships, or health feel unstable, money often steps in to perform reassurance.

And sometimes spending is about resentment. Quiet resentment. The kind that builds when you give more than you receive, carry more than your share, or postpone your own needs for too long. In those moments, spending becomes one of the few places you feel entitled to take up space.

None of this makes you irresponsible.

It makes you human.

Before you decide that your spending needs discipline, ask a different question: *What is my money trying to help me survive right now?* Relief? Control? Comfort? Belonging? Rest? When you name the underlying need, spending becomes information instead of something to police.

This is why value-based spending works best when it's paired with honesty. You don't fix spending by shrinking your life. You fix it by making your life more supportive, so money doesn't have to compensate for what's missing.

When your days are better aligned, spending often changes without effort. Not because you restricted yourself, but because you no longer need money to fill the same gaps.

For Ann, the breakthrough wasn't restraint. It was alignment.

That insight changed how I think about spending and how I teach it.

Spending with purpose isn't about spending less. It's about spending in a way that reflects your values *and* your capacity. When your life is misaligned, money often tries to compensate. When your life becomes more supportive, spending naturally follows.

Here's how I approach value-based spending now.

First, I named my core values with honesty. Family, health, learning, service, and independence. Not aspirational words, but the things I wanted my money to protect and grow.

Then I looked at my recurring expenses through that lens to try to understand them. If something didn't align, I asked two questions: *Is this meeting a real need?* And *Is this helping me build the life I want, or helping me tolerate one that doesn't fit?*

That distinction matters.

From there, I built three spending categories that offered flexibility without chaos.

- The first is **needs**. These are the expenses that keep life safe and functional: housing, food, healthcare, basic transportation.

- The second is **values-driven wants**. This includes spending that actively supports the life you're building. Experiences with family. Learning. Health. Meaningful travel. Support for causes or businesses you care about.

- The third is what I call **joy margin**, a small, intentional amount of discretionary spending that carries no guilt. This isn't about the number. It's about permission. When joy has a place, it stops sneaking in sideways.

These categories shifted spending from something I controlled to something I *designed*.

Inside the Empowered Sisterhood, this is often where women experience their first real shift. Not because they're given stricter rules, but because they're finally given language. When spending reflects values instead of stress, guilt begins to loosen its grip.

Two small practices helped cement this for me.

The first is the "before you click" pause. Sixty seconds before any nonessential purchase. Just long enough to ask: *Does this support something I care about, or is it a momentary escape?*

The second is the twenty-four-hour rule for impulse buys. Write it down. Screenshot it. Revisit it tomorrow. Most cravings pass. The ones that don't usually deserve intention.

Over time, I also began paying attention to the emotions behind spending. Comfort. Reward. Relief. Pride. Naming the emotion didn't eliminate the desire, but it turned it into information instead of impulse.

And finally, I automated what mattered. A portion of my income goes directly into a values fund, which is money specifically set aside for the things I say matter most. That one move changed spending from reactive to intentional almost overnight.

Here's where I want you to start—not with a spreadsheet but with awareness.

Write down the three values that matter most to you right now. Then complete this sentence for each one:

This month, I will spend in a way that honors _______.

Next, look at where your money has actually been going. Sort it into three buckets: needs, values-driven wants, and joy margin. If something doesn't fit any of those, don't judge it. Ask what it's been responding to.

If your spending feels high, ask a deeper question before cutting anything: *What in my life feels unsustainable right now?* Like Ann, you may discover that the spending isn't the root. It's the signal.

You will drift back into autopilot sometimes. That doesn't undo the work. Each return to intention builds trust.

If you want deeper momentum, try a ninety-day season focused on value-based spending. Adopt the pauses. Re-allocate a portion of discretionary spending toward your values. Track alignment, not perfection.

Over time, consistent, values-led choices add up in ways that may surprise you, reshaping not just your bank balance, but your sense of purpose.

In the next chapter, we'll turn to saving for stability and learn why liquidity and planning are not cold concepts but rather emotional safeguards that create freedom when life changes.

Spending isn't about discipline. It's about design. And when your money supports your life instead of compensating for it, everything else gets easier.

Chapter 6

Saving for Stability and Building Your Foundation

THE DOOR SHUTS SOFTLY behind me, and the silence is almost frightening in its certainty. In that stillness, money is either a source of panic or a source of peace. For years, I treated savings like a rainy-day rumor. Nice to have, rarely urgent, something you could postpone until the next pay period.

Then life handed me a real storm. A surprise medical bill, a car that needed three grand in repairs, and a job transition that felt unstable enough to rattle the walls of my confidence. In those moments, I finally understood what stability feels like when you're standing on solid ground you deliberately built.

I started with a simple practice. I counted what I truly needed to feel safe for the next six months, then a little more for unexpected storms. I opened a dedicated savings account, automatic transfers humming in the background like a steadfast heartbeat. It wasn't glamorous, but it was real.

And when a payment came due—co-pays, utility spikes, a deductible or two—I didn't panic. I had a cushion whispering, "We've got you." The relief wasn't loud, but it was undeniable. Saving wasn't a moral test or a restriction. Saving was a permission slip to breathe, to plan, and to live with the knowledge that I could handle what's coming next without breaking the life I'm building.

What savings really protects isn't just your bank balance. It protects your nervous system. When you have liquidity, your decisions change. You don't say yes as quickly out of fear. You don't stay in situations that drain you simply because you can't afford to leave. You respond instead of react. Savings creates the internal permission to pause, to think, and to choose. It widens your sense of possibility long before it ever shows up as a financial milestone.

That's why saving isn't about deprivation or discipline. Saving is about building enough internal and external stability to live your life without constant vigilance.

The real obstacle isn't whether you should save versus invest. It's the emotional pull of immediate gratification paired with a stubborn, backward-facing belief about debt. So many of us were trained to worship debt as a sign of ambition. Buy now, pay later, and prove you're future-ready by flashing more stuff.

But the truth I've learned, and I've watched my clients learn, is that liquidity is not a luxury. It's a safeguard that makes every other risk you take more sustainable.

There's also the misalignment between the big dream and the small daily habits that keep it afloat. We tell ourselves, "I'll save when I get a raise," or "I'll pay down debt after this next project," but life doesn't wait for perfect moments. Emergencies don't announce themselves with banners.

The fear of scarcity can paralyze us into inaction, while the lure of fancy goals without a foundation can bankrupt momentum before it begins. The result is a budget that promises security in theory but collapses in practice. High gains on paper, low peace of mind in the middle of a stressful month.

Another layer: Debt is not inherently evil. It's a tool. The problem arises when debt absorbs your future. If you're paying high-interest rates, or if debt consumes cash that should be funding emergencies and opportunities, you're tilting the entire life you're trying to build. It's a cultural habit. We need to reframe debt as risk management, savings as the backbone, and investments as the bonus that only thrives when you're not living on the edge.

The breakthrough for me, and the clients I coach, was realizing that stability isn't a single action. It's a three-part system that can coexist with growth. I named it as a practical, repeatable framework. Three buckets that keep your life steady while you pursue bigger dreams.

The Liquidity Bucket: Emergency Savings

This is your safety net. The rule isn't "as much as you can." It's "enough to weather the next six to twelve months of necessities and the next big life event without fear." I start with a minimum target—three to six months of essential living expenses—and then I build a buffer for irregular incomes or seasonal costs. Automate, automate, automate!

A fixed amount every payday goes here, no excuses. The goal is to remove the friction between money earned and money saved, so you don't have to make a binary choice between today's comfort and tomorrow's security.

The Debt-Management Bucket

Here we face the hard truth. If you carry high-interest debt, you're pulling forward costs from the future into today. I don't advocate debt denial; I advocate debt discipline. We adopt a payoff approach that fits the person. The avalanche method for those who want to minimize interest, or the snowball method for momentum and motivation. The key is to create a clear plan with milestones, so debt isn't a weight you carry forever but a schedule you own and finish.

The Growth Bucket: Investing

Once liquidity is in place and debt is under control, we carefully shift more of the available cash into growth. This isn't "never touch cash again." It's about preserving options—a portion of investments accessible in a reasonable time horizon, a portion allocated to retirement, and a portion reserved for strategic opportunities. The objective is to let money work without sabotaging security. We tailor this bucket to risk tolerance and life stage, always ensuring liquidity where needed.

Alongside these buckets, I built two practical rituals that anchor behavior. First, the "three-bucket budget mapping" ritual. Each month, I map every dollar into Liquidity, Debt, or Growth before anything else. If something lands outside those buckets, it's a red flag.

Second, I schedule a quarterly "reset," a calm, honest check-in with myself about whether the buckets still reflect my life and goals. The act of labeling helps me see where I'm compromising or gaining ground, and it keeps shame out of the conversation.

Let me tell you about Maya.

She came to me carrying what she called "the guilt of two lives." On one side was the mortgage and the credit card balance—debt she'd been chipping at for years, always feeling behind. On the other was the pressure to keep things looking fine. Vacations on credit. Dinners out because her friends were going. A quiet, grinding sense that she was performing stability without actually feeling it.

When we sat down together, the first thing that surprised her was how little she knew about where her money was going. Not because she was careless but because she'd been so focused on putting out fires that she'd never stopped to build a system.

We started with the Liquidity Bucket. Six months of essential expenses, set aside in a dedicated account. It felt impossible at first. The number was bigger than anything she'd ever saved intentionally. We started small. An automatic transfer every payday, no bigger than a restaurant dinner. She didn't feel it leave her checking account, but she watched the cushion grow.

Once that foundation started taking shape, we moved to the Debt Bucket. Maya was someone who needed momentum more than math. We started with the smallest balance, not the highest interest rate. Watching that first account hit zero changed something in her. It wasn't the money. It was the proof that she could finish something.

The Growth Bucket came last, and it was modest. A steady drip into a broad-market index fund, nothing flashy. But it was the first time Maya had ever put money somewhere that wasn't about surviving the month. It was about building a future she could picture.

Within eight months, something had shifted. Not just in her accounts but in how she carried herself. She stopped apologizing for saying no to things that didn't matter. She stopped lying awake wondering if she could cover an unexpected bill. She told me once, quietly, "I didn't know what it felt like to not be afraid of money. I think I always assumed that's just how it is." It isn't. And she was living proof.

Saving for stability isn't a destination. It's a discipline that reshapes how you live. The three-bucket system gives you a living blueprint you can rely on when the world shifts. An emergency fund to keep anxiety in check, a disciplined debt plan to free up future cash, and a growth strategy that honors your long-term goals without starving today's joy.

If you're starting from scratch, here's what I want you to do this week. Sit down with a quiet hour and figure out what it costs to keep your life running each month. The basics: rent or mortgage, groceries, healthcare, the things you can't live without. Then multiply that number by six. That's your first target, the number that will let you breathe when life gets loud. It doesn't have to feel reachable right now. It just has to feel real.

Next, take an honest look at your debt. Write it all down, every balance, every interest rate. You don't need to pay it all off this week, but you do need to see it clearly. Then pick a payoff method that fits how you're wired. If you want to minimize what you pay in interest over time, start with the highest rate first. If you need the quick wins to keep yourself motivated, start with the smallest balance. Neither approach is wrong. The only wrong move is ignoring it.

And then—and this is the one that changes everything—set up automatic transfers. One amount to your emergency fund. One to your debt payoff. One smaller amount to growth. Let the system do the work for you, so you're not white-knuckling it every pay period. Once it's automatic, it stops being a decision and starts being a habit.

A few weeks in, take a step back and look at the bigger picture. Are there expenses coming up in the next six to twelve months that you haven't planned for? A tuition bill, a medical cost, a trip that matters to you? If so, start reshaping the buckets now, before the surprise arrives.

And once a quarter, sit down with yourself or someone you trust, and ask: *Is this still working?* Adjust what needs adjusting. Celebrate what's working. That's it. That's the whole system.

In the next chapter, we'll turn to the art and science of investing for growth—how to move from stability to empowerment by building a portfolio that aligns with your values and your life. We'll explore risk in a way that respects both your heart and your head, and I'll share how to translate liquidity and debt discipline into the courage to invest boldly, yet prudently.

Chapter 7

Invest for Freedom: Your Money Working for You

Not long after I left equity research to build my own practice, I understood investing better than almost anyone in the room and still felt quietly terrified about my own financial future.

I had spent years in that world. Analyzing companies. Building models. Writing reports that moved markets. I understood how compounding worked. I could explain risk-adjusted returns to a roomful of executives without breaking a sweat. The mechanics of investing were not a mystery to me. They never had been.

But understanding something professionally and trusting it personally are two very different things.

When I left a stable salary to start Intentional Wealth Partners, the ground shifted beneath me in ways I hadn't fully anticipated. I had three kids. I had a business that was brand new and not yet proven. I had a deep, intellectual confidence in how markets work and a much quieter, much more honest fear about whether any of that mattered when the paycheck stopped being automatic.

Those early years were hard. Not dramatically hard. Quietly hard. The kind of hard where you keep showing up, keep building, and keep believing, but in the back of your mind, there's a steady, low hum of: *Is this going to work? Am I going to be OK? Are we going to be OK?*

I did what I knew how to do. I contributed. I invested. I set things in motion and tried not to look too closely, because looking too closely meant confronting the gap between what I knew intellectually and the uncertainty I felt in my body. Even with all my training. Even with everything I understood about how wealth is built over time.

Then one morning, sometime in the first few years after I'd started the practice, I sat down to do a routine review of my accounts. Nothing prompted it. No crisis. No milestone. I just opened the statements and started looking at the numbers.

And something had changed.

My investments had grown. Not because I'd done anything new or clever. Not because I'd timed the market or picked the right stock. They had grown because I had put money in, time had passed, and the money had done what money does when you let it work. It was making money. Quietly.

Without me pushing it. Without me earning it or hustling for it or proving anything.

I sat with that for a while. The feeling wasn't pride. It wasn't excitement. It was relief.

Deep, almost physical relief. Like a breath I'd been holding for years had finally come out. Something was working. Not because of what I was doing every day, but because of what I had done, months and years before, and then trusted enough to leave alone.

That moment didn't teach me anything I didn't already know. I understood compounding. I understood the math. What it taught me was something I couldn't have learned from a model or a report or a decade of equity research.

It taught me what it feels like to trust it.

And that, the feeling, not the knowledge, is what changes everything.

I see this gap between knowing and trusting all the time. It's one of the most common things women bring into my office, though they rarely name it that way. They come in feeling like they've been "good" with money but still uneasy. They've saved consistently. They've contributed to their retirement plan. They've done the responsible things. And yet something feels off. Something feels incomplete.

Kim was one of those women.

She had a solid job, a steady paycheck, and a 401(k) she'd been contributing to for years. On the surface, she was doing everything right. But when we started looking more closely, the gaps became obvious, and they were the kind of gaps that don't show up on a performance review.

First, she wasn't getting the full employer match because no one had ever clearly explained how it worked. She thought contributing "something" was enough. She didn't realize that stopping short of the full match meant she was leaving part of her compensation on the table every single year.

Second, the money she was contributing was invested extremely conservatively. Most of it sat in stable-value and bond-heavy options because those choices felt safer. She'd never been told how her investments worked, and in the absence of clarity, fear filled the gap.

But before I tell you what we changed, let me tell you what Kim's life felt like.

She checked her 401(k) balance maybe once a year, usually when her employer sent a statement in the mail. And when she did look, she felt a quick spike of something she couldn't quite name. Not fear, exactly. More like a low hum of *I don't understand this*, and I'm afraid that matters.

She'd read articles about investing. She'd listened to podcasts in the car. But none of it stuck, because none of it connected to her life. It all sounded like it was written for someone else—someone younger, someone without kids, someone who had time to think about the future instead of trying to survive the present.

She did what felt safest. She contributed what she'd been told to contribute. She picked the options that sounded the least risky. And then she looked away, because looking too closely felt like opening a door she wasn't sure she was ready to walk through.

When I asked her what she thought investing was supposed to feel like, she said, "Honestly? I thought it was supposed to make me nervous."

That stopped me. Because I recognized it as something I had felt myself. The belief that investing meant enduring discomfort. That nervousness was the price of admission. That if it didn't feel hard, you were probably doing it wrong.

You don't need to love investing. You just need to trust the system you build.

Kim wasn't trying to beat the market. She wasn't chasing hot stocks or early retirement fantasies. What she wanted was freedom. The kind that comes from knowing that a job change wouldn't unravel her life, that a market downturn wouldn't send her into a panic, that her future self was quietly being taken care of. She wanted her money to support her life, not loom over it.

We slowed everything down.

We started with the basics: how the 401(k) match worked and what it meant in real dollars over time. When I showed Kim the numbers, what she was leaving on the table every single year by not contributing enough to capture the full match, her expression changed. It wasn't shock, exactly. It was more like recognition. She hadn't known. No one had ever explained it to her in a way that made it land.

We adjusted her contributions so she was capturing the full match—an immediate, guaranteed return she'd unknowingly been missing. Then we looked at her investment allocation and talked about what her money needed to do over the next twenty and thirty years. Not in abstract terms, but in the context of her life. Her kids. Her goals. The version of herself she was growing into.

Nothing dramatic changed overnight. But something important shifted. She stopped seeing investing as a test she might fail and started seeing it as an opportunity that could quietly work in the background of her life. Her shoulders dropped. Her questions changed. She wasn't asking, "Is this risky?" anymore. She was asking, "Does this support the future I want?"

That's when it clicked for me in a deeper way. Investing isn't about returns in isolation. It's about returns that preserve your time, your values, and your sense of agency. It's about money doing the heavy lifting so you don't have to.

The biggest barrier to investing well is almost never a lack of intelligence. It's fear, noise, and misalignment. We're surrounded by extreme messages—promises of effortless wealth *or* warnings that one wrong move will ruin everything. Investing gets framed as a competitive sport or a moral referendum on how brave or savvy you are.

For many women, there's another layer. We've been conditioned to be cautious, to avoid mistakes, to defer to experts. We do what feels safe. We contribute to the 401(k) because we're told we should. We pick conservative options because we don't want to mess it up. And then we don't look too closely, because looking might bring up questions we're not sure how to answer.

Over time, the combination of under-contributing, overly conservative investing, and avoidance can quietly erode freedom. Not because anyone did anything wrong, but because no one ever stopped to connect investing to real life.

A quick, honest note: All investing involves risk. Markets go up and down, outcomes are never guaranteed, and uncertainty is part of the process. The goal here isn't to eliminate risk. It's to understand it, plan for it, and build a structure you can live with through the ups and downs.

My own shift didn't come from discovering a new strategy. It came from changing how I think about investing altogether. I stopped teaching it as a way to win and started teaching it as a way to support a life. Over time, I landed on three principles that consistently help women move from anxiety to confidence. Whether they're employees contributing to a 401(k), business owners investing profits, or somewhere in between.

The first principle is **foundations first**.

Before growth, we build stability. I think of investing in layers. The foundation is your core: low-cost, broadly diversified investments designed to grow steadily over time without unnecessary complexity. This is where simplicity is a strength. Boring is not a flaw. Boring is durable.

For many people, this core lives inside a workplace retirement plan like a 401(k). That's not a bad thing. But it only works if you're using it intentionally, contributing enough to capture the full match, and choosing investments that align with your time horizon, not just your fear level on a given day.

The **growth layer** comes next. This is where your money participates more fully in opportunity, calibrated to your actual capacity for risk. Growth isn't about recklessness. It's about giving your future self more options. And it only works when it's built on a foundation that lets you stay invested during inevitable market swings.

The final layer is **tax awareness**. This is the quiet factor that often gets overlooked. Taxes, fees, and account structure matter more over time than most people realize. Small inefficiencies add up. Thoughtful planning, choosing the right accounts, understanding when and how money is taxed, and paying attention to fees helps preserve what you earn so your money can do more work for you.

The goal of this structure isn't to maximize returns in any single year; it's to maximize reliability. To create a plan that keeps moving forward even when life gets complicated.

The second principle is **aligning risk with capacity**, not just comfort.

Risk tolerance, how you feel about market ups and downs, matters. But risk capacity, what you can withstand financially without derailing your life, matters more. I've worked with women who felt emotionally comfortable with risk but couldn't afford a significant loss because they were supporting children, parents, or both. I've also worked with women who had strong balance sheets but felt anxious simply because no one had ever explained what their investments were doing.

This is where an Investment Policy Statement becomes so helpful. It's not a technical document meant to impress anyone. It's a personal anchor. It answers a few simple questions: *What am I investing for? How much volatility can I realistically tolerate without panicking? What do I do when the market drops or when my life changes?*

Putting those answers in writing changes everything. Decisions become calmer. Headlines lose their grip. You stop reacting and start responding. The plan becomes your compass, not a fire alarm.

The third principle is **discipline over drama**.

Even the best investment plan fails without consistency. Markets don't reward perfection. They reward patience. This is why automation matters so much. Automatic contributions remove emotion from the equation. Regular rebalancing keeps your portfolio aligned without requiring constant attention. Periodic reviews, quarterly, not daily, allow you to adjust thoughtfully instead of reacting impulsively.

I tell clients this all the time. You don't need to watch your investments to make them work. You need to trust the system you've built. Time is the most powerful ingredient in investing, and discipline protects it.

Kim learned this firsthand. About six months after we made her initial adjustments, the market dipped. Not dramatically, but enough that she noticed. She called me, and I half expected the familiar anxiety I'd heard from so many others. Instead, she said something quiet and steady: "I looked at it. I felt nervous for about thirty seconds. And then I remembered why it was set up the way it was. And I just let it be."

That was the moment I knew something had genuinely shifted for her in her portfolio and in her relationship with money itself. She had moved from avoidance to engagement. From confusion to clarity. From the belief that investing was supposed to make her nervous to something quieter and steadier.

Trust.

A few months after that, she told me she'd sat down with her kids and explained how her 401(k) worked. Not because they'd asked. Because she wanted them to see it, wanted them to know that their mother understood her own financial life, and that understanding it didn't have to feel scary.

"I spent years pretending I had it figured out," she said. "Now I do. And it feels so much lighter than the pretending ever did."

That's what investing for freedom looks like when it's working. Not fearlessness. Not perfection. Just a quiet, grounded sense that your money is doing something meaningful and that you're the one who made it happen.

If investing has ever felt like the part of money you'd rather not think about, stay with me here. You don't need to predict markets or memorize acronyms. Start with this instead:

Write down what you want your money to make possible.

Not what it should do.

Not what someone else told you it's supposed to do.

What you want.

Maybe it's the option to step back from work earlier than planned. Maybe it's the ability to leave a job that no longer fits. Maybe it's helping your kids without sacrificing your own future. Maybe it's simply knowing you'll be OK.

Put a rough timeline next to those goals. This is the beginning of your Investment Policy Statement—your personal guide for every investing decision that follows.

Then, look at what you already have. Open your accounts. If you have a 401(k), check whether you're getting the full match. Look at how your money is invested and what you're paying in fees. You don't need to change anything today. Seeing clearly is the work right now.

If what you see feels overly conservative, overly complicated, or just confusing, that's information, not failure. Start with one adjustment. One question. One step.

Then automate what you can and let the system do its job. Revisit your plan periodically, not to chase headlines but to make sure it still supports the life you're building.

And finally, leave room for possibility. Not everything needs to fit neatly into a retirement account. If there's a future opportunity, a business idea, a meaningful project, allow yourself a small pocket of flexibility. Enough to stay curious. Not so much that it destabilizes what you've built.

Investing isn't about being fearless. It's about being intentional.

In the next chapter, we'll talk about Giving with Your Heart, how generosity fits into an intentional wealth plan without compromising your security. We'll explore what it means to give from a place of connection rather than obligation, and how to build a practice of generosity that sustains you instead of draining you.

You don't need to know everything to invest well. You just need a plan that respects your life.

Chapter 8

Giving with Your Heart: Generosity as Intentional Wealth

GROWING UP, I LEARNED a Hebrew word that changed how I understood what it means to give: *tzedakah*. It's often translated as *charity*, but that word doesn't quite capture it. Charity implies a gift offered from abundance, something optional, something that flows one direction. *Tzedakah* is different. It's rooted in justice. It says that when you have more than you need, giving isn't just kindness, it's responsibility. Not because someone is beneath you, but because you are connected to one another. A community that doesn't care for its members isn't truly secure.

That idea stayed with me as I built my financial planning practice and as I sat with women navigating every kind of transition: divorce, reinvention, caregiving, rebuilding after loss. Because what *tzedakah* makes clear is something most financial advice misses entirely. Generosity and security are not opposites. When giving is grounded in values rather than guilt, it doesn't weaken your foundation. It strengthens it.

But I've also seen the other side.

I've watched women give until they were depleted. Stretch until they were anxious. Say yes long after it stopped feeling aligned. They told themselves this was what it meant to be good, to be generous, to be loving. But underneath, resentment quietly built. Fear crept in. The giving that once felt meaningful began to feel heavy.

That's not generosity. That's self-abandonment wearing the language of virtue.

The goal of intentional giving is to give in a way that reflects who you are, what you value, and the life you're building without compromising your own stability or peace of mind.

Let me ask you something gently: When you think about giving, what do you feel first?

If the answer is guilt, pressure, or obligation, you're not alone. Many women have been taught that generosity means going last, that taking care of others should come at the expense of our own safety. That wanting limits is selfish.

Such beliefs quietly erode both generosity and security.

When Giving Loses Its Grounding

Without structure, generosity tends to swing between extremes. We give impulsively when emotion is high, then pull back entirely when life feels expensive or overwhelming. Or we commit to amounts that don't reflect our real capacity, then carry anxiety every time a bill comes due.

Another common pattern is performative giving—donations made because it feels expected, because it avoids discomfort, or because saying no feels harder than saying yes. Over time, this kind of giving creates quiet resentment, not connection.

Intentional generosity asks a different question: *What kind of giving supports both my values and my future?*

That question changes everything.

Three Lanes of Intentional Giving

To make generosity sustainable, I encourage clients to think about giving across three distinct lanes, not to divide money evenly but to bring clarity.

Immediate impact

Giving that happens close to home to individuals, families, or causes where you can see and feel the effect.

Strategic giving

Support for organizations aligned with long-term outcomes and shared values.

Legacy giving

Forward-looking generosity that reflects the values you want to carry beyond your lifetime.

Naming these lanes doesn't restrict generosity; it focuses it.

Andrea's Story

Andrea came to me about a year after her divorce. Her finances were stable, but something felt unfinished. For most of her adult life, she had tithed—not out of obligation, but identity. It connected her to her values and to something larger than herself.

During her marriage, that practice slowly faded through quiet resistance and the desire to avoid tension. Eventually, giving became something she defended rather than celebrated and then something she set aside entirely.

When she finally named how much she missed it, she also admitted her fear: *What if giving again puts my future at risk?*

We didn't rush. We built a plan that reflected her actual capacity, not her past habits or someone else's expectations. When she resumed giving at an amount that felt sustainable, something settled inside her.

"I didn't realize how much of myself I'd tucked away," she told me. "This feels like coming back."

She wasn't giving more than before. In some ways, she was giving less. But for the first time, it was entirely hers, chosen freely, without apology or anxiety. That distinction made all the difference.

That's intentional giving. It's not dramatic. It's grounded in what feels right for the giver.

Where Boundaries Belong

This is also where boundaries matter most, especially in relationships with adult children.

I think of a client I'll call Marianne.

Marianne had raised three children largely on her own after a late-life divorce. She was proud of how resilient they were and terrified of watching them struggle. Whenever one of her adult children hit a financial rough patch, she stepped in. Rent shortfalls. Credit card balances. Emergency expenses that weren't truly emergencies.

Each time felt small. Reasonable. Loving.

But when we sat down together, the pattern became clear. Marianne was dipping into retirement savings she'd worked decades to build. She was lying awake at night worrying about her own future and then telling herself that worry was selfish.

"I just want them to be OK," she said.

What she hadn't named yet was the financial and emotional cost. She felt resentful, exhausted, and quietly scared. Her generosity was no longer rooted in choice and was driven by fear of disappointing her children or being seen as unsupportive.

We didn't start by cutting anything off. We started with clarity.

What support helped her children grow?

What support kept them dependent?

What did she need to feel safe twenty years from now?

When Marianne finally set her first boundary, saying no to covering a recurring expense, she cried afterward. Not because she felt cruel, but because it went against everything she'd been taught about love.

A few months later, she told me something that surprised her.

"My son figured it out," she said. "It was hard. But he did. And our relationship feels clearer now."

Boundaries are not a withdrawal of love. Boundaries **are** love.

They say: *I care enough about you to support growth, not just comfort.*

They say: *I'm protecting a future where I don't become a burden to you.*

They say: *This support is intentional, not automatic.*

When generosity isn't paired with boundaries, it quietly transfers anxiety instead of building independence. Parents become financially strained and emotionally depleted. Adult children miss the opportunity to build confidence and capability.

Sustainable generosity requires clarity about what help truly helps and what simply postpones growth.

Giving That Lasts

Intentional giving also considers *how* you give. Thoughtful planning allows generosity to continue year after year without destabilizing your financial life. Whether that means adjusting timing, choosing tax-efficient strategies, or aligning giving with income fluctuations, the goal is the same: generosity that strengthens rather than strains.

I've seen this transform families. Children included in conversations about values. Giving modeled as a thoughtful choice, instead of an obligation. Money used not just to accumulate, but to express who a family is and what they stand for.

Where to Begin

Start small. Not with numbers, but with clarity.

Write one sentence for each lane:

- One way you want to give now

- One cause or organization you want to support over time

- One value you want your money to express beyond you

Then ask yourself one honest question: *Does my current giving support my life, or does it quietly undermine it?*

There's no right answer, only awareness.

Generosity is not something you earn after you're "done" building wealth. It's part of how intentional wealth is lived. When giving is aligned with values, supported by structure, and held by boundaries, it becomes one of the most meaningful expressions of a life well lived.

And when it's done with intention, generosity doesn't drain you. It roots you.

Chapter 9

Mindset Shifts That Change Everything

I ONCE SAT ACROSS from a client who had everything most people associate with success.

A senior title.A six-figure income.Respect in rooms she had worked hard to earn a seat in.

On paper, she was doing more than fine.

But as we talked, her voice softened. She leaned in and said, almost apologetically,"I don't feel like I deserve any of this."

She wasn't careless with money.She wasn't irresponsible. She wasn't failing.

She was living inside a story she didn't know she had inherited.

That story told her that wealth was fragile. That wanting more ease was risky. That security could disappear if she relaxed for even a moment. She stayed vigilant. She minimized her wins. She talked herself out of opportunities that might have given her more freedom because she didn't believe she was allowed to have that freedom.

That conversation stayed with me because it clarified something essential: **Mindset isn't a side note in your financial life.** It's the lens through which every decision passes.

Change the lens, and everything else changes with it.

I know this personally. There were years when talking about money made my chest tighten. When negotiating felt like asking for permission. When every setback, no matter how ordinary, felt like confirmation that maybe I wasn't built for this. I had the knowledge. I had the credentials. What I didn't yet have was a deep belief that I was allowed to build something that worked for me.

Through my own experience and through years of sitting with women navigating divorce, loss, career shifts, caregiving, burnout, and reinvention, I've learned that most money beliefs aren't chosen.

They're absorbed.

They come from the tone in which money was discussed. From what was celebrated. From what was warned against. From what was never talked about at all.

They sound like:

- Be careful.

- Don't want too much.

- Money causes problems.

- You should just be grateful.

These stories often came from somewhere real. From people trying to survive. From generations doing the best they could with what they had. But just because a belief once protected someone else doesn't mean it deserves to run your life now.

Most of the time, the challenge isn't that you don't know what to do with money. It's that an old story gets activated before you even realize you're making a choice.

Maybe you hesitate to negotiate, even though you know you should. Maybe investing feels scarier than it "should." Maybe you downplay success or feel guilty wanting more stability or ease.

That's not a discipline issue. That's usually a belief issue.

For women especially, this runs deep. Many of us were taught—explicitly or not—to keep things smooth, to avoid being demanding, to take care of everyone else first. We learned to be competent without being visible and capable without being confident.

When discomfort shows up around money, it doesn't mean you're doing something wrong. It often means you're brushing up against conditioning that was never meant to serve you forever.

Left unexamined, these beliefs create invisible limits. You can have the income, the opportunity, the plan, and still feel stuck. Often because you're trying to build a new life using an old internal rulebook.

The shift comes when mindset stops being treated as something to fix and starts being treated as something to notice.

Where Mindset Actually Shows Up

Mindset rarely announces itself as a belief. It shows up as a reaction.

It's the pause before you check your bank balance. The tightness in your chest when an unexpected expense appears. The instinct to justify a purchase you don't need to justify or to avoid one you can afford.

I often tell clients: **If money feels emotional, that's not a problem to solve. It's information.**

One woman I worked with delayed opening her investment accounts for years. This had nothing to do with not trusting the markets, but somewhere along the way, she absorbed the belief that if she looked too closely, she'd discover she'd already made a mistake. Avoidance felt safer than confirmation.

Another client negotiated every other area of her life with confidence but froze when it came to asking for flexibility at work. Her belief wasn't "I don't deserve more." It was quieter than that. "If I ask, I might disrupt something that feels stable."

These patterns don't come from laziness or lack of intelligence. They come from stories about safety, worth, and belonging.

When you start noticing where you hesitate, rush, or avoid, you will find the places where mindset is quietly steering the wheel.

And once you see that, you have options.

A Practical Way to Work with Mindset

This isn't about dramatic breakthroughs but rather gentle, honest engagement.

First, notice the story.

Write down the money messages you remember hearing growing up. The casual lessons. The offhand comments. The assumptions no one questioned. Seeing them on paper removes their invisibility.

Then, question it gently.

Is this always true?Has it ever not been true?Do I know people whose lives contradict this belief?

You're not arguing with yourself. You're creating space.

Then, choose something new. Not a forced affirmation but rather a believable next thought.

"I'm bad with money" becomes "I'm learning how to make intentional decisions."

"Wanting more is selfish" becomes "Wanting stability and ease is reasonable."

"I'll mess this up" becomes "I can take one thoughtful step."

New beliefs don't need to feel fully true. They just need to feel lighter.

Finally, reinforce them with small actions. Beliefs don't change through motivation; they change through **evidence**.

Evidence comes from opening your accounts without panic. From following through on a small plan. From making one decision aligned with your values and surviving it.

This is also why environment matters—who you listen to, what messages you let in, whether money is treated as a taboo or as something meant to support your life.

And it's why support matters. Beliefs loosen faster when they're spoken out loud instead of carried privately.

Mindset Doesn't Work Alone

Mindset is powerful, but it doesn't operate in isolation.

Without clarity, mindset work stays abstract.Without values, belief has no direction.Without strategy, confidence has nowhere to land.Without action, insight never becomes e mbodied.Without support, even the strongest mindset gets tired.

This is why mindset work isn't about fixing yourself. It's about creating enough internal space to use the tools you already have. When belief and structure work together, change stops feeling like willpower and starts feeling like alignment.

I've seen what happens when this work is done with patience.

A woman who believed debt was her permanent condition questioned that story and paid off over $40,000 because she stopped believing she was someone debt belonged to.

Another client, a senior leader, had never negotiated her salary, not once in over a decade. She practiced the conversation. She sat with the discomfort. And when she finally asked, she was met with an immediate yes. The belief dissolved the moment it was tested.

None of them changed overnight. They changed because they stopped believing the story that said change wasn't for them.

Tolerations: The Quiet Costs You Stop Noticing

There's one mindset shift that often surprises people because it doesn't sound like a money issue at first.

I call it **tolerations**.

Tolerations are the small things you live with even though they drain you. These aren't big, dramatic problems. They're the everyday irritations you've learned to accept because addressing them feels inconvenient, uncomfortable, or not worth the effort. They show up quietly.

The subscription you forgot to cancel. The bill that's slightly higher than it should be, but not high enough to trigger action. The drawer that never closes. The recurring expense you resent every month but keep paying, anyway. The commitment you dread every time it appears on your calendar.

Individually, none of these feel urgent. Collectively, they create constant background noise.

Each toleration carries a **quiet cost**.

Sometimes that cost is financial with money leaking out in small, unnoticed ways. More often, the cost is emotional, leading to irritation, resentment, low-level stress, and a sense that things are slightly out of control.

And here's the part most people miss. Tolerations don't just drain energy; they teach you something about yourself.

Every toleration sends a subtle message of *This is fine*, even when it isn't. Over time, those messages stack up. You stop trusting your discomfort. You normalize things that don't fit. You tell yourself it's not a big deal and then wonder why you feel depleted or stuck.

This shows up in money more than almost anywhere else.

You tolerate:

- fees you don't fully understand

- accounts you avoid looking at

- spending that doesn't reflect your values

- income arrangements that feel unfair but familiar

You tolerate these things because addressing them feels harder than living with them.

Here's what's important to understand: **Clearing tolerations builds confidence faster than almost anything else** because it restores agency.

When you remove a toleration, you send yourself a different message: *I notice when something isn't working. I respond. I don't have to live with quiet discomfort.*

That belief matters.

I've watched women make meaningful shifts simply by canceling one subscription, renegotiating one bill, fixing one small thing they'd been stepping around for years. The action itself is small. The internal impact is not.

If this resonates, start here.

Make a short list, no more than five items, of things you're tolerating right now. Include money-related ones and life-related ones. Don't judge the list. Just notice it.

Then choose **one**.

Not the hardest one.Not the most dramatic one.The one that feels slightly annoying and completely doable.

Fix it. Cancel it. Address it. Clean it up.

Pay attention to how that feels.

Most people expect relief.What they don't expect is momentum.

Tolerations are often the first place we relearn that our comfort matters, our attention matters, and our money doesn't have to quietly compensate for what we've stopped questioning.

This isn't about perfection. It's about responsiveness.

And responsiveness, noticing and adjusting instead of ignoring and enduring, is one of the most important mindset shifts you'll make with money.

For many women, tolerations are deeply tied to a fear of disappointing others. We tolerate situations that drain us because saying no feels heavier than carrying the discomfort. This shows up powerfully around money. Over-giving, undercharging, and absorbing costs that aren't ours to carry because approval has quietly been linked to safety.

Why Endurance Gets Mistaken for Strength

For many women, tolerating discomfort has been framed as maturity, kindness, or strength. We learn early that smoothing things over keeps us safe. That being agreeable avoids conflict. That carrying the weight quietly is more admirable than naming what's not working.

Endurance becomes a skill. We endure unfair expectations. We endure unclear agreements. We endure financial arrangements that feel slightly off but socially acceptable.

Endurance stops being situational and starts becoming identity. We don't ask whether something fits; we ask whether we can survive it. And because we *can*, we assume we should.

Money is often where this pattern becomes visible first.

You tolerate fees because calling feels uncomfortable.Y ou keep paying for something that no longer serves you because changing it feels like making a fuss.You continue supporting others financially even when it strains you because setting a boundary feels like rejection.

None of this happens because you lack confidence. It happens because you've been rewarded for making things easier for everyone else.

The problem is that endurance doesn't scale.

What you tolerate today quietly shapes what you believe you deserve tomorrow. Tolerations gradually teach your nervous system that discomfort is normal and responsiveness is optional. You stop trusting the signals that say *This isn't working anymore.*

Clearing tolerations isn't about becoming rigid or selfish. It's about retraining yourself to respond when something feels misaligned instead of absorbing the cost silently. Each small correction restores a little more self-trust. Each boundary reinforces the belief that your comfort and clarity matter too.

This is why tolerations sit at the intersection of mindset and action. They're not abstract beliefs. They're lived decisions. And when you start gently and consistently addressing them, you don't just change your finances. You change the story you're telling yourself about what kind of care you're allowed to require.

If you learned that harmony mattered more than honesty or that being "good" meant being agreeable, tolerations can feel like kindness rather than avoidance. They teach damaging lessons that your comfort is optional, your needs are negotiable, and your future self will somehow make it work.

Naming this pattern is part of recognizing that tolerations often protect relationships in the short term and erode self-trust in the long term. Money is frequently where this tradeoff becomes visible first.

Give This a Try This Week

You don't need to overhaul anything.

Notice one money belief that feels heavy.Question it gently.Choose a softer replacement.Clear one small toleration.Talk about money with someone you trust.

That's enough.

Mindset work isn't a breakthrough moment. It's a relationship you build with yourself over time. Old stories will resurface. When they do, that doesn't mean you've failed.

It means you've noticed. And noticing is where change begins.

Chapter 10

From Intention to Action: Bringing It All Together

BY THE TIME MOST women reach this point, they don't lack insight.

They know what they *should* be doing. They've read the articles, listened to the podcasts, maybe even worked with an advisor before. They understand the basics. They can explain the concepts. They recognize themselves in the stories.

And yet, something still doesn't move.

That gap between understanding and follow-through is where good intentions quietly stall.

I've sat with women who could explain how markets work but avoided opening their accounts. Women who had thoughtful plans but hadn't taken a single step in months. Women who were capable, responsible, and deeply motivated and still felt stuck.

For a long time, I assumed the solution was more structure. A clearer system. A better plan.

But the longer I did this work, the clearer it became: The problem wasn't missing information; it was missing support for change.

Change asks something different of us than learning does.

Learning can happen quickly. It fits neatly into a podcast episode or a chapter in a book. Change, on the other hand, asks for repetition. It asks for patience. It asks for a container strong enough to hold us when motivation fades and life gets loud.

Without that container, even the best ideas slip back into the background.

Why Action Breaks Down

Action doesn't fail because people don't care. It fails because life is full.

Our days are crowded with real responsibilities—work, caregiving, relationships, health, and the constant pull of what needs attention right now. Financial decisions rarely feel urgent until something breaks. They get postponed or relegated to "when things calm down."

And things rarely calm down.

There's also the emotional weight. Money carries identity, fear, history, and old stories. Taking action can feel risky even when the step itself is small. Doing nothing often feels safer than doing something imperfect.

For women especially, there's another layer. Many of us were taught to manage quietly. To be competent without being visible. To put others first and ourselves last. Planning for our own future can feel indulgent, even when we know it's necessary.

We wait. We gather information. We promise ourselves we'll start soon.

And *soon* keeps moving.

What creates movement isn't pressure or discipline. It's momentum, accountability, support, and working together.

Momentum Comes from Small, Repeatable Actions

We tend to imagine change as something dramatic. A big decision. A bold declaration. A moment where everything clicks.

In reality, change usually happens quietly.

It happens when a small action is repeated often enough that it becomes familiar. When fear is replaced with neutrality. When money stops feeling charged and starts feeling workable.

I call these micro-actions. They're small by design. Small enough to feel doable on a busy day. Meaningful enough to create forward motion.

A micro-action might look like:

- Opening your banking app and simply looking

- Automating one transfer so it no longer depends on willpower

- Spending ten minutes once a week reviewing where your money went

- Writing down one money decision you've been avoiding and naming why

None of these will transform your financial life on their own. But repeated consistently, they do something powerful.

They rebuild trust with yourself.

And that trust, the quiet confidence that you can look, decide, adjust, and continue, is what makes larger decisions possible.

A Tale of Two Approaches

I once worked with two women who started in nearly identical places. Both felt overwhelmed. Both wanted clarity. Both were eager to "get it right."

The first tried to do everything at once. She rewrote her budget, opened new accounts, read three books, and created a detailed plan over a single weekend. By the following month, she was exhausted. When life interrupted, as it always does, she fell behind and quietly abandoned the plan because the system required a version of her that didn't exist consistently.

The second chose one small action. She set up a weekly ten-minute check-in with her money. That was it. No overhaul. No pressure. Just presence. A month later, she added one automated transfer. A few weeks after that, she scheduled a conversation she'd been avoiding.

Six months in, she hadn't "done everything." But she was still engaged. And that made all the difference.

Accountability Is About Witness, Not Pressure

Most women I work with don't need more discipline. They already hold themselves to high standards.

What they need is accountability that feels safe.

Accountability isn't about being monitored or corrected. It's about being seen. It's about having a place to say, "Here's what I tried. Here's what worked. Here's where I got stuck," without shame.

When progress is witnessed, even imperfect progress, it becomes easier to continue. When it's invisible, it's easy to abandon.

This is why structured check-ins matter—daily, weekly, monthly, whatever rhythm fits your life. Not to judge outcomes, but to stay in relationship with the process.

Consistency matters more than intensity.

Community Is What Makes Change Sustainable

Money change is not a solo sport. Isolation is one of the most underestimated barriers to financial growth. When we believe everyone else has it figured out, we hide. When we hide, we stagnate.

Community breaks that pattern.

When you hear someone articulate a fear you thought was uniquely yours, something softens. When you watch someone else take a step you've been avoiding, possibility becomes concrete. Not aspirational—*real*.

This is why I created the Empowered Sisterhood, a space where money conversations are normal. Where progress is shared. Where shame loses its power because it's no longer private.

Change sticks when it's supported.

The 90-Day Intentional Money Reset

If this book has helped you see your money differently, the next question isn't *What should I do next?*

It's *How do I stay with this long enough for it to matter?*

The 90-Day Intentional Money Reset is designed to answer that question. Not as a rigid program but as a season.

Ninety days is long enough to build momentum and short enough to feel manageable, especially when the focus isn't perfection, but consistency.

The first thirty days are about orientation.Seeing clearly without judgment.Noticing patterns.Understanding what matters to you right now.

The middle thirty days are about steadiness.Aligning small habits with your values.Automating what you can.Creating a little more breathing room.

The final thirty days are about forward motion.Taking one meaningful step, investing, planning, deciding, that reflects the confidence you've been building quietly all along.

This reset isn't about fixing yourself or your finances. It's about staying connected to the work when motivation dips. About giving yourself structure without pressure. About practicing intention instead of just thinking about it.

If you'd like a companion to walk alongside you as you do that, you can find it at.

Why 90 Days Works

Ninety days is intentional. It's long enough for new habits to move from effort into familiarity, but short enough that it doesn't feel overwhelming or indefinite. Most people overestimate what they can change in a week and underestimate what steady attention can do over a season.

Ninety days gives you space to experiment without pressure, to notice patterns without judgment, and to build trust with yourself through repetition. It allows insight to turn into practice and practice to turn into confidence because you've stayed with the work long enough to feel grounded inside it. By the time ninety days pass, money no longer feels like something you're avoiding or managing from a distance. It feels like something you're in relationship with—something you can look at, adjust, and engage with calmly.

Where to Start

You don't need a grand plan to begin. Start small.

This week, choose one simple action and repeat it for a few days. Let it be manageable. Let it be almost boring. Let it be something you can keep.

Maybe it's a morning balance check.Maybe it's writing down your values and noticing where your money already supports them.Maybe it's scheduling fifteen quiet minutes on Sunday evening to look at the week.

Starting counts. Coming back counts. And when you drift, as everyone does, return without judgment.

That's the work.

You don't need to do this all at once.You don't need to do it alone.

The bridge between intention and action isn't built in a day. It's built the same way everything meaningful is built: slowly, deliberately, and with support.

And you're already on it.

Conclusion: Your Money, Your Story, Your Life

THE MORNING I FINISHED the first full draft of this book, I didn't immediately feel relief.

Instead, I felt still. Not empty. Not finished. Just quiet in a way that told me something important had settled.

For a long time, I thought this book was about helping women "do money better." Make smarter decisions. Avoid mistakes. Feel more confident.

But sitting there that morning, what became clear was this book was never really about money.

It was about permission.

Permission to question the rules you inherited.Permission to define success on your own terms.Permission to stop performing financial competence and start building financial confidence.Permission to honestly trust yourself.

Money is simply where all of that shows up.

I think back to earlier versions of myself. The woman who believed that bigger numbers would eventually quiet her anxiety. The woman who worked harder, earned more, spent more, and still felt like something was missing. The woman who thought security was something you reached if you just stayed vigilant long enough.

I also think about the women I've sat across from for years. Women in the middle of divorce, career reinvention, caregiving, grief, or quiet dissatisfaction they couldn't quite name. Women who came to me convinced they were behind, broken, or bad with money. However, their reality was quite different. They were simply navigating systems and expectations that were never designed for their full lives.

What changed things for them wasn't a single insight or strategy.

It was being given space to slow down. To see clearly. To ask better questions. To stop measuring themselves against someone else's life.

That's the work you've been doing as you moved through these pages.

And it matters more than you might realize.

This Was Never About Getting It Right

If there's one idea I hope you carry forward, it's that there is no version of this work where you arrive and stay there forever.

Your life will change. Your needs will shift. Your values will evolve. Your financial picture will move through seasons of clarity, complexity, and recalibration.

That doesn't mean you're failing. It means you're living.

The goal was never to give you a rigid plan that only works if nothing unexpected happens. The goal was to give you a **way of orienting yourself** when things do change.

That's why the Intentional Money Method isn't a checklist. It's a language. It's a language, built on six pillars that were never meant to be mastered, only returned to. Clarity. Values. Mindset. Strategy. Action. Support.

When something feels off, you now have a way to ask:

Where do I need clarity? What values are asking to be honored? What story is shaping this decision? What structure would actually support me here? What small action could help me regain momentum? Who can walk with me through this?

Those questions don't expire. They grow with you.

You Are Already More Capable Than You Think

Many women finish a book like this and immediately ask, *"Am I doing enough?"*

Let me answer that gently.

You don't need to overhaul your financial life to be making progress. You don't need to implement everything at once. You don't need to feel confident every day.

The fact that you stayed with this book, that you reflected, questioned, noticed, and paused, already tells me something important about you.

You're paying attention. Attention is where agency begins.

From there, everything else becomes possible.

I've seen women who started with nothing more than a weekly ten-minute check-in eventually build stability they never believed was available to them. I've watched women who once avoided their accounts become calm, thoughtful decision-makers. I've seen women who believed money would always feel scary describe, years later, a quiet sense of trust they didn't know existed.

Those shifts didn't happen because those women were extraordinary; they happened because they stayed engaged.

The Long View

One of the most overlooked aspects of money work is how *long* it lasts. This isn't a sprint. It's not even a season. It's a relationship that unfolds over decades.

There will be years where money feels easy and years where it feels tight. There will be times when you feel proud of your decisions and times when you wish you'd chosen differently. There will be moments when you need to act quickly and others when waiting is the wisest move.

None of that disqualifies you from having a healthy relationship with money.

What matters is not perfection, but repair. Not certainty, but responsiveness. Not control, but trust built over time.

If you take nothing else from this book, remember that you are allowed to learn as you go.

If You Want Support Along the Way

Some readers will close this book and move forward on their own, quietly integrating what resonated. That's a valid and powerful path.

Others will want structure. A rhythm. A place to return to when life pulls them away from their intentions.

That's why the **90-Day Intentional Money Reset** exists.

Not as a requirement. Not as a fix. But as a companion.

It's designed for women who want help consistently staying with the work—a place to practice clarity, values alignment, mindset awareness, and small actions in real time, with support that understands real life.

If that sounds useful to you, it's there at whenever you're ready.

And if now isn't the right time, trust that too. This work doesn't disappear just because you're not actively focused on it.

A Gentle Way to Begin (or Continue)

If you're unsure what comes next, let it be simple.

Tomorrow, look at your money. Just look. The next day, name one thing you want your money to support this month. The day after that, talk about money with someone safe.

That's it.

No declarations. No pressure. No overhaul.

Small moments of engagement, repeated, are what build confidence.

A Blessing for the Road Ahead

As you step forward from these pages, I want to leave you with this.

May you meet your financial life with curiosity instead of judgment.

May you give yourself permission to change your mind as your life evolves.

May old stories soften as new ones take root.

May your plans feel supportive rather than restrictive.

May your actions be sustainable, your support steady, and your confidence quietly earned.

May you remember, especially on hard days, that you are not behind, you are becoming.

Your money story is not finished.It's not fixed.It's not something you need to prove.

It's something you get to live.

And you are already doing that, one intentional step at a time.

About the Author

Leah Hadley is a financial planner, Certified Divorce Financial Analyst (CDFA®), Master Analyst in Financial Forensics (MAFF™), Accredited Financial Counselor (AFC®), and trained mediator. She is the founder and CEO of Intentional Wealth Partners and Intentional Divorce Solutions, where she helps women build financial lives that reflect their values, not just their net worth.

Leah created the Intentional Money Method™ after years of sitting with women in the middle of life's most disorienting transitions: divorce, reinvention, caregiving, and the quiet reckoning of realizing the plan they'd been following no longer fit. Her work combines rigorous financial expertise with deep respect for the emotional complexity of money, meeting clients where they are rather than where they think they should be.

She is the founder of The Empowered Sisterhood, a community where women talk about money honestly and build wealth together. She also hosts two shows: *Intentional Money Moves*, a live weekly program, and the *Intentional*

Divorce Insights podcast. A graduate of Bryn Mawr College, Leah is a committed advocate for women's leadership through organizations including NAWBO.

She lives in Cleveland, Ohio, where she is a proud adoptive mother of three.